Kansas

impressions

photography by **Steve Mulligan** *and* **Michael Snell**

FARCOUNTRY
PRESS

Right: Cedar bluffs border a wheat field in Decatur County in northeastern Kansas. STEVE MULLIGAN

Title page: Welda Prairie Preserve occupies 128 acres in Anderson County in eastern Kansas. STEVE MULLIGAN

Front cover: In this classic Kansas scene, a windmill in Ellis County is silhouetted by a brilliant prairie sunset. STEVE MULLIGAN

Back cover: Sunflowers are native to Kansas and grow well in the state's hot, dry summers. MICHAEL SNELL

ISBN 10: 1-56037-392-X
ISBN 13: 978-1-56037-392-6
Photography © 2006 by Steve Mulligan and Michael Snell
© 2006 Farcountry Press

For more information about our books write Farcountry Press, P.O. Box 5630,
Helena, MT 59604; call (800) 821-3874; or visit www.farcountrypress.com.

Created, produced, and designed in the United States. Printed in China.

10 09 08 07 06   1 2 3 4 5

Located in Abilene, President Dwight D. Eisenhower's hometown, the Eisenhower Center is a five-building complex on twenty-two acres. Five limestone pylons honor the former president's parents, David and Ida Eisenhower, their six sons, America's Veterans, American democratic ideals, and Dwight D. Eisenhower, Army general and thirty-fourth president of the United States. MICHAEL SNELL

Left: The Kaw Mission State Historic Site is situated on the northern end of the Riverwalk, a winding path along the banks of the Neosho River at Council Grove in east-central Kansas. At the southern end of the Riverwalk is the eight-foot-tall bronze statue of a Kaw warrior, *The Guardian of the Grove*. MICHAEL SNELL

Below: South of the community of Timken is the National Bohemian Cemetery, the final resting place for many immigrants who came to the small town from Bohemia in the late nineteenth century. MICHAEL SNELL

Above: One of the nation's most unusual tombs, the Davis Memorial in Mount Hope Cemetery in Hiawatha was built by John Milburn Davis between 1931 and 1934 "in sacred memory" of his wife, Sarah. The memorial comprises eleven lifesize marble and granite statues depicting the couple. MICHAEL SNELL

Right: This house in Atchison is the birthplace and early childhood home of aviator and noted early female pilot Amelia Earhart. Now the Amelia Earhart Birthplace Museum, the property features personal memorabilia and tours. Earhart, born on July 24, 1897, disappeared mysteriously over the Pacific Ocean during a flight in 1937. MICHAEL SNELL

Left: In the 1880s, a Colorado miner named Charles Griffee carved several caves in the Dakota sandstone in Ellsworth County. They were named the Faris Caves, after the family who purchased the property from Griffee. MICHAEL SNELL

Far left: The spectacular badlands in north-western Kansas are the Arikaree Breaks, and were carved by water running through the fine, silty soil called loess. MICHAEL SNELL

Above: A western meadowlark, the state bird of Kansas, belts out a song. DONALD M. JONES

Right: The Elk River, a tributary of the Verdigris River in southeastern Kansas, tumbles down Elk Falls. STEVE MULLIGAN

Following pages: The nighttime skyline of Wichita, the largest city in Kansas, is reflected in the Arkansas River. MICHAEL SNELL

Right: Every other year in Lindsborg, also known as Little Sweden, folks gather to celebrate their Scandinavian heritage at Svensk Hyllningsfest. The festival features art, crafts, ethnic food, folk dancing and music, a parade, smörgåsbord, and other entertainment. MICHAEL SNELL

Below: Two young dancers show off their skills at the Fiesta Bullwhacker, an annual celebration in Olathe that includes historic reenactments, Mexican and European music, dancers, crafts, food, children's activities, and stagecoach rides. MICHAEL SNELL

Above and right: Waterfalls grace the countryside, including this one on Wolf Pen Creek in Bourbon County (above) and another on Rock Creek in Pottawatomie County (right), both in northeastern Kansas. STEVE MULLIGAN

Facing page: Stately cottonwood trees shade the rolling terrain in Dickinson County in east-central Kansas. STEVE MULLIGAN

Right: This sculpture of a horse and rider at the western edge of Marysville in the Hall Brothers Pony Express Park celebrates the legacy of the Pony Express riders. Depicted is Jack Keetley, the first rider to travel west on the initial run from Marysville to Sacramento on April 3, 1860. MICHAEL SNELL

Below: Designated a National Historic Landmark in 1961, the historic Hollenberg Pony Express Station in Washington County in northeastern Kansas was established in 1858 by Gerat J. and Sophia Hollenberg as a stop for travelers on the Oregon–California Trail. The Pony Express began using it as a station in 1860. STEVE MULLIGAN

Left: This sculpture, *Dreamers Awake* by Tom Otterness, graces the grounds of the Wichita Art Museum. Established in 1915, it is the largest museum in Kansas. MICHAEL SNELL

Below: A statue of the Tin Man from *The Wizard of Oz* stands in a field near the town of Howard—perhaps still searching for a heart? In the classic 1939 film based on the L. Frank Baum book *The Wonderful Wizard of Oz*, the character of Dorothy was taken by a tornado from her Kansas farm to the magical land of Oz. STEVE MULLIGAN

Right: A long pool leads to a tiered Roman fountain surrounded by eight columns in Mission Hills' Verona Columns Park, which was created by Herbert Hare in 1925. The 3,000-pound, twelve-foot-tall columns were brought to Kansas from Verona, Italy. In the center of the grouping of columns is a marble urn, also from Italy.
MICHAEL SNELL

Far right: The University of Kansas Museum of Anthropology in Lawrence makes its home in historic Spooner Hall, designed in the Romanesque Revival style by Kansas City architect Henry van Brunt and dedicated in October 1894.
MICHAEL SNELL

Right: The sunflower is the state flower of Kansas, which is nicknamed The Sunflower State. STEVE MULLIGAN

Facing page: Goodland, the heart of the sunflower industry, is the home of this eighty-foot easel, which displays a twenty-four- by thirty-two-foot replica of Van Gogh's *Sunflowers.*
MICHAEL SNELL

Visitors can see the inner workings of an old flour mill at the McPherson County Old Mill Museum in Lindsborg on the banks of the Smoky Hill River. MICHAEL SNELL

The annual Kansas State Fair takes place in Hutchinson, site of the first official Kansas State Fair in 1913. MICHAEL SNELL

Right: Snowfall blankets yuccas growing on the Arikaree Breaks.
STEVE MULLIGAN

Far right: In 1995, this 1860s church was moved from its original site in Sproxton, England, to the Baker University campus in Baldwin City. The church was then renamed the Clarice L. Osborne Memorial Chapel in honor of the wife of the project's patron.
MICHAEL SNELL

Left: The historic Drinkwater and Schriver Flour Mill was built in 1875 on the Cottonwood River at Cedar Point in east-central Kansas. STEVE MULLIGAN

Below: Evening primrose shows off its bright-yellow blooms. STEVE MULLIGAN

Above: Deep Creek forms a lovely waterfall as it drops over a limestone outcropping near Manhattan in the northeastern portion of the state.
STEVE MULLIGAN

Right: South of Galena is Schermerhorn Park, a scenic fifty-square-mile area referred to as the "Kansas Ozarks." STEVE MULLIGAN

Left: The Missouri River forms Kansas's northeastern boundary with Missouri.
STEVE MULLIGAN

Facing page: It's spring, and trees along this placid stretch of the Elk River are beginning to flower.
STEVE MULLIGAN

Right, top: Completed in 1894, the historic Atchison Post Office was constructed of cottonwood limestone. It features towers at its southeast and southwest corners and an arched entryway.
MICHAEL SNELL

Right, bottom: The Rosedale Arch in Kansas City stands in tribute to the soldiers of World War I and was dedicated in 1923. The design of the arch was based on the Arc de Triomphe in Paris. A later addition to the monument was dedicated to honor the soldiers of subsequent wars and conflicts.
MICHAEL SNELL

Facing page: The Breidenthal Biological Reserve in the Baldwin Woods near Baldwin City protects ninety acres of eastern deciduous forest. This stream provides habitat for many species of mosses and liverworts that are rare in the Great Plains. STEVE MULLIGAN

Above: Henry's Candy Kitchen, in Dexter in southern Kansas, has been tempting locals and visitors alike with its homemade confections since 1956. MICHAEL SNELL

Left: Kansas wheat fields, such as these in Morris County in the east-central part of the state, are a patchwork of color and texture. STEVE MULLIGAN

Right: A covered wagon at the Red Buffalo Ranch serves as a reminder of pioneer days in Kansas. The ranch occupies 8,000 acres near Sedan at the eastern edge of the Flint Hills.
STEVE MULLIGAN

Below: Bison graze at the Konza Prairie Biological Station, an 8,600-acre research site that is named after the Konza Indian tribe. Bison are the state animal of Kansas. STEVE MULLIGAN

Left: Established as a mission and school for Kaw Indian children in 1851, the two-story limestone Kaw Mission is now a state historic site that details the culture of the tribe and the area's history. MICHAEL SNELL

Below: Pioneer grave markers are found along the emigrant trails that cross the state. This headstone and simple message mark the grave of pioneer Sarah Keyes at Alcove Spring in the northeastern portion of the state. STEVE MULLIGAN

Right: Located near the community of Lyons, this intaglio in the shape of a serpent is believed to be from A.D. 1200 to 1300, and was created by a Native American tribe of the region. Approximately 160 feet long, the serpent figure varies in width from 4 to 10 feet.
STEVE MULLIGAN

Far right: The Konza Prairie, in the Flint Hills of northeastern Kansas, is characterized by steep-sloped hills with shallow limestone soils. Because the soil is unsuitable for cultivation, the Konza Prairie is now the largest remaining area of unplowed tallgrass prairie in North America.
STEVE MULLIGAN

Above: The bronze statue *El Capitan* commemorates the 1875 to 1885 Texas cattle drives to Dodge City. MICHAEL SNELL

Left: Dodge City—setting for the popular Western TV show *Gunsmoke*—was established in 1872 to supply goods and services to soldiers and wagon trains at nearby Fort Dodge. These re-created storefronts depict a Front Street of yesteryear. MICHAEL SNELL

Right: The Kansas Museum of History in Topeka interprets the colorful history of the state, with exhibits of Western artwork and historical artifacts. Pictured is the train named after Cyrus K. Holliday, one of the founders of Topeka.
MICHAEL SNELL

Far right: The Kansas Cosmosphere in Hutchison features a collection of U.S. space artifacts second only to the National Air and Space Museum, as well as the largest collection of Russian space memorabilia outside of Moscow. Exhibits include the actual *Apollo 13* command module and a Vostok spacecraft.
MICHAEL SNELL

Left: Blazing star flowers and grasses carpet the verdant Konza Prairie. STEVE MULLIGAN

Below: The wind bends a Siberian elm on the Flint Hills Prairie. STEVE MULLIGAN

Right: President Dwight D. Eisenhower grew up in this home in Abilene; his family lived there from 1898 until 1946. Eisenhower graduated from Abilene High School in 1909. MICHAEL SNELL

Below: Rust-colored lilies display their showy blooms. STEVE MULLIGAN

EISENHOWER
HOME

1898 - 1946

Left: Built in 1923, the Marsh Arch Bridge, known as "Rainbow Bridge," lies between Riverton and Baxter Springs on Route 66.
MICHAEL SNELL

Far left: More than 200 of these huge sandstone concretions are spread across the landscape at Rock City, south of Minneapolis in central Kansas. Formed when Dakota sandstone became cemented together with calcium carbonate, these formations are the largest and most numerous of their kind in the world.
MICHAEL SNELL

Right: Located in Liebenthal in central Kansas, St. Joseph's Kirche is one of the loveliest churches in the state. Members of the parish constructed the church of native stone from 1902 to 1905. MICHAEL SNELL

Below: A soldier left this inscription on the barracks at Fort Larned, which was established in 1859 in western Kansas near the midpoint of the Santa Fe Trail. STEVE MULLIGAN

Left: Clear Pond in central Kansas is part of the McPherson Valley Wetlands and an excellent place for bird-watching. STEVE MULLIGAN

Facing page: Located six miles northeast of Great Bend, Cheyenne Bottoms is a 41,000-acre lowland that is the home of several threatened and endangered species, including whooping cranes, peregrine falcons, least terns, and piping plovers. STEVE MULLIGAN

Right: In northwestern Kansas, yellow prince's plume brings a splash of color to the chalk badlands known as Little Jerusalem—the largest exposure of Niobrara chalk in the state. STEVE MULLIGAN

Below: These limestone outcroppings are evidence of the unique geological history of Big Basin Prairie Preserve, which occupies 1,818 acres in the Red Hills of south-central Kansas. STEVE MULLIGAN

Left: A full moon peers through Keyhole Arch at Monument Rocks, a series of large chalk formations in west-central Kansas that is rich in fossils. STEVE MULLIGAN

Below: The Prairie Center, a 300-acre nature sanctuary west of Olathe in northeastern Kansas, includes forty-five acres of virgin tallgrass prairie. STEVE MULLIGAN

Right: Looking like sand dunes, hills of harvested grain sorghum, or milo, await transport near Quinter in western Kansas. In the United States, grain sorghum is primarily used as livestock feed. STEVE MULLIGAN

Below: Castle Rock, in the Smoky Hills region of northwestern Kansas, is a large limestone pillar nearly seventy feet in height. Travelers along the Butterfield Overland Dispatch route (Overland Trail) used the formation as a landmark. STEVE MULLIGAN

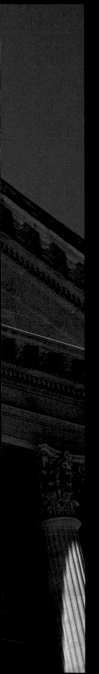

Above: Sunlight illuminates an ethereal scene in stained glass at the Topeka and Shawnee County Public Library. The window was removed from the Woodward, a castle-like chateau built in 1923 in Topeka. Now a bed and breakfast, the Woodward was built for Chester and Frederica Woodward to resemble an authentic English estate. MICHAEL SNELL

Left: Construction on the Kansas State Capitol in Topeka took place in three stages, beginning in 1866 and ending in 1903. The capitol measures 304 feet from ground level to the top of the cupola. MICHAEL SNELL

Right: The Milford Nature Center in Junction City educates the public on the state's wildlife and habitats and is located near the Milford Reservoir in west-central Kansas's Flint Hills.
MICHAEL SNELL

Far right: In 1938, the Public Works Administration built the Amelia Earhart Memorial Bridge, a long-span steel-truss bridge across the Missouri River at Atchison.
MICHAEL SNELL

Left: The dramatic Buffalo Soldier Monument in Leavenworth stands as a tribute to the U.S. Army's Buffalo Soldiers, the African-Americans who served in the 9th and 10th Cavalry Regiments.

MICHAEL SNELL

Far left: The Kansas State University Gardens are the home of numerous plant collections, as well as several specialty gardens such as the Cottage, Butterfly Zoo, and Native/Adaptive Plant Gardens.

MICHAEL SNELL

Right: The Chikaskia River, a tributary of the Salt Fork Arkansas River, originates in Kansas and flows south into Oklahoma.
STEVE MULLIGAN

Far right: Sunset casts a warm glow on the chalk badlands of Little Jerusalem in west-central Kansas.
STEVE MULLIGAN

Left: Cement sculptures of Adam and Eve stand at the gate to the Garden of Eden in Lucas in north-central Kansas. Retired-schoolteacher and Civil War–veteran Samuel Perry Dinsmoor began building the garden in 1907 at the age of sixty-four. He completed it twenty-two years later. The site is listed on the National Register of Historic Places and welcomes more than 10,000 visitors each year. MICHAEL SNELL

Below: Bison make their home on the mixed-grass prairie of Big Basin Prairie Preserve. MICHAEL SNELL

Right: Southwest of the community of Traer in the northwestern part of the state stands Elephant Rock, an eroded limestone outcropping that was used as a landmark by emigrants. STEVE MULLIGAN

Below: Prairie Dog State Park occupies 1,150 acres on the shores of Keith Sebelius Reservoir in western Kansas. From the mounds around the burrows, black-tailed prairie dogs watch for predators such as coyotes, prairie falcons, golden eagles, and badgers. STEVE MULLIGAN

A storm brews in the skies above this windblown wheat field in Sumner County. Nearly twenty percent of Kansas residents are employed in jobs related to agriculture. MICHAEL SNELL

Re-enactors
show what life
was like on the
wagon trains
as emigrants
traveled west
through Kansas
MICHAEL SNELL

Steve Mulligan

Landscape photographer Steve Mulligan runs a stock photography business from his home in Moab, Utah. He travels extensively, spending a great deal of time photographing the Kansas landscape with his large-format 4x5 camera. *Outdoor Photographer* magazine named Steve a Master Landscape Photographer in 1999. His work was featured in the Kodak Professional Photographers' Showcase at Epcot Center, and his recent book of black-and-white photography entitled *EarthWorks* was chosen as photography book of the year by *Black and White Photographer* magazine.

Pictured are Steve and his daughter Alyssa.
www.mulliganphotography.com

Michael Snell

Michael Snell graduated from the University of Kansas in 1985 with a degree in visual communications and spent the next fourteen years working as an art director in the advertising industry. Michael taught at Washburn University before becoming a freelance travel photographer and graphic designer in 1997. Since then his images have appeared in *Kansas!* magazine, the *Kansas Getaway Guide, Midwest Living, Michigan Travel Ideas, Country Living, Destinations,* Disney's *Family Fun, AAA Home & Away, AAA Midwest Living, AAA Journeys,* the *Los Angeles Times Magazine,* and *National Geographic* publications.

Michael's photographs have appeared in several books, including *Forever Kansas!,* the *This Land is Your Land* series, *Uniquely Kansas, Driving Across Kansas, Monster Nation,* and Mobil and Michelin travel guides.

Michael has won numerous awards from the Society of American Travel Writers and the North American Travel Journalists Association. He is a native Kansan and currently lives in Topeka with his wife, Sally. Together they own Shade of the Cottonwood, a creative services company.

www.shadeofthecottonwood.com